# Paleo Ba
# and
# Dessert Recipes

## 53 Delicious Paleo Baking Recipes of the Week

*By*

*Patrick Smith*

ISBN-10: 1502770679
ISBN-13: 978-1502770677

# Contents

# Preamble: Is this Paleo?

All ingredients used in this book are either paleo or commonly considered to be acceptable for the paleo diet. The latter means that most people agree with it, while only a minority disagrees. Each ingredient has been rigorously checked to ensure this fact, but as you know, there are rare cases where opinions diverge.

If you spot an ingredient that you personally do not consider paleo, feel free to replace it as you see fit. Better yet, check appropriate paleo ingredient lists on the Internet to see for yourself whether an ingredient you are unsure about is okay.

The purpose of this recipe book is to replace the usual ingredients for pastries with paleo alternatives, including paleo chocolate, paleo cheese, and natural sugars. Since pastries use at least *some* ingredients that are rarely used in cooking, you may be unfamiliar with their paleoness, so let us have a quick look at a few of them.

### Raisins
Raisins are just grapes that are sun-dried or dehydrated. They are natural foods without additives or added sugar. However, they are high in natural sugars and have lots of calories, so they should not be over eaten.

### Chocolate (cocoa)
Chocolate is made from cocoa, a natural ingredient that itself is paleo. Dark chocolate is paleo as well, because it contains very high amounts of cocoa. Milk chocolate, on the other hand, is likely not to be considered paleo, but opinions vary on this matter.
As you will see in the first recipe of this book, paleo chocolate can easily be home made from coconut milk and cocoa powder.

### Coconut
Coconut ingredients of any kind (milk, butter, oil, flour, powder, sugar) are healthy and natural. In fact, they are eaten in very large amounts by indigenous islanders in the pacific, who are known to

5

be the healthiest people in the world. People in tropical places like this have been eating coconuts for thousands of years. This provides a tremendous opportunity for paleo dieters, since so many ingredients are made from coconut. You can bake with coconut flour, use coconut sugar to sweeten pastries, make chocolate with coconut milk and grease pans with coconut oil.

**Vanilla extract**
Vanilla is an orchid that grows in Africa, where humans originally came from. This means that vanilla has always been readily available to our species.
Judging from the literature out there, vanilla extract is regarded as a paleo ingredient, even though it contains alcohol. Since it is concentrated, you will be using such small amounts of it (like ½ tsp) that it does not even matter to the biochemistry of your body and can be ignored.

**Pumpkin Pie Spice**
This is paleo, simply because it is made from paleo ingredients, such as cinnamon and ginger.

**Honey**
Like any brown bear knows, honey is made by bees and readily available in nature, which makes it a telltale paleo food. In its raw form, it has many health benefits and comes with natural sugars that can serve as a replacement to white/brown sugar.

However, most honey available in supermarkets today has been processed at high temperatures and is devoid of most nutrients. Processed honey may or may not be paleo, as opinions vary in this case. The best way to go about it is to buy raw honey from a local farmer or to find an online store that sells bio-foods.

Cavemen had to work hard to find honey and did not have much available at any time, so make sure you do not eat it every day. For baking, we will need honey in small amounts to add sweetness and extra taste.

# Section 1: Chocolate recipes

## 1. Dark Chocolate

Paleo chocolate made easy. There are many possible variations to this recipe, if you add orange zest, almond butter, dried coconut, chopped nuts, cinnamon, or other ingredients. The chocolate is ready in a little more than an hour.

½ cup **cocoa powder**
½ cup **coconut oil**
½ tsp **vanilla extract**
3 tbs **raw honey**
1 pinch of **sea salt**

Makes 8 servings
Calories: 139 per serving

In a pan, melt coconut oil over medium-low flame. Stir in cocoa, vanilla, honey and salt. Whisk to blend.

Pour the mixture into a candy mold or rimmed plastic tray. Refrigerate for an hour.

Enjoy!

## 2. Coco-Choco Cake

This is a simple yet satisfyingly dense chocolate cake that uses coconut ingredients. Top with your favorite frosting. It is ready in 45 minutes.

1 cup **coconut flour**
¾ tsp. **baking soda**
¾ cup **cocoa powder**
9 large pastured **eggs**
1 cup **raw honey**
¾ cup **coconut oil** (melted)
1 ½ tbs **vanilla extract**
¾ tsp. **salt**

Makes 24 servings
Calories: 145 per serving

Preheat oven to 350°F (180 °C).

In a bowl, combine flour, cocoa, salt and baking soda. Mix well.

In a separate bowl, beat eggs until fluffy. Add the rest of the ingredients and mix to blend. Slowly pour this mixture into the first bowl and mix until a batter is formed. Add water if needed to attain desired consistency.

The batter should be enough for 2 round cakes at 9 inches (23 cm). Fill 2 cake pans lined with parchment paper and bake for about 30 minutes, or until toothpick comes out clean when inserted at the center. Alternatively, use cupcake forms to make cupcakes.

Remove from oven and let cool on wire rack.

Enjoy!

# 3. Coconut-Almond Chocolate Cake

This is a two-layered chocolate cake with frosting. It is done in 45 minutes.

Cake:
½ cup **cocoa powder**
4 pastured **eggs**
1 cup **almond flour**
¼ cup **coconut flour**
½ cup **arrowroot powder**
1 tsp **baking soda**
1 cup **raw honey**
¼ cup **coconut oil**
2 tsp **vanilla extract**
½ tsp **salt**

Frosting:
¾ cup **dark chocolate chips**
   or self-made **paleo chocolate**
1 tbs **raw honey**
6 tbs **coconut milk**

Makes 16 slices
Calories: 266 per slice

Preheat oven to 350°F (180 °C) and grease two 9 inch (23 cm) springform pans. Line bottom with parchment paper.

In a bowl, combine dry ingredients. Whisk in wet ingredients and mix until desired consistency is attained. Transfer batter to the prepared pans and bake for about 30 minutes, or until a toothpick comes out clean when inserted at the center.

For the frosting: In a bowl, melt dark chocolate chips (or self-made paleo chocolate from recipe 1) over a hot water bath or in a double boiler, if you have one. Once melted, add coconut milk and honey, then whisk until smooth.

Remove from heat and let cool to room temperature. It may take ½ hour. Make sure the mixture does not get hard and can still be poured. Spread the frosting on top of one cake, followed by the second cake to create a two-layered cake. Alternatively, you can use the frosting to cover both cakes and serve them separately.

Enjoy!

# 4. Chocolate Applesauce Cake

This Paleo chocolate cake is baked in about 40 minutes.

5 pastured **eggs**
1 cup **applesauce**
¼ cup **raw honey**
1 tbs **vanilla extract**
¼ cup **coconut oil**
1/3 cup **coconut flour**
¾ cup + 2 tbs **cocoa powder**
1/3 cup **tapioca flour**
½ tsp. **baking soda**
½ tsp. **baking powder**
¼ tsp. **salt**

Makes 12 servings
Calories: 142 per serving

Preheat oven to 325ºF (160ºC). Lightly grease a Bundt cake pan. In bowl, whisk eggs using a hand mixer. Add the rest of the wet ingredients, ending with coconut oil. Set aside.

In another bowl, combine flour with the rest of the dry ingredients. Mix well. Slowly pour into the wet mixture and mix using hand mixer.

Drizzle cocoa powder all over the prepared Bundt pan. Shake to remove excess powder. Transfer batter into the pan and bake for about 40 minutes.

Remove from the oven allow to cool for 20 minutes. Run a knife around the edge of the pan to loosen the cake. Place a plate or wire rack over the pan and flip it over to remove the cake. Cool and cut into 12 slices.

# 5. Hot Chocolate with Coconut-Almond Milk

A thick and creamy hot chocolate treat for extra cold winter days. It can be used as a glazing for the cupcakes in recipe 4 of section 4.

1 cup **coconut milk**
2 cups **almond milk**
1 tsp **vanilla extract**
2 tbs **cocoa powder**
4 oz. (110g) **dark chocolate chips**
  or self-made **paleo chocolate**

Makes 4 servings
Calories: 126 per serving

In a medium sized pot, combine all ingredients but the chocolate. Heat over medium-low flame and mix to blend.

Add the dark chocolate chips or self-made paleo chocolate (from recipe 1). Simmer and constantly stir over low heat for about 2 minutes, or until fully blended. Serve hot.

Enjoy!

## 6. Paleo Mousse Chocolate

This recipe is a real treat and can be used for a wide variety of pastries. It is used in recipe 2 of section 6 for banana-chocolate ice cream.

1 cup **hazelnuts**
¼ cup **cocoa powder**
2 tbs **coconut oil**
½ cup **almond milk**
2 tbs **coconut sugar**
½ tsp **vanilla extract**

Makes: 1 cup
Calories: 120 per serving

Preheat oven to 350°F (180°C).

Line a baking sheet with parchment paper. Place hazelnuts on the sheet and roast for about 10 minutes. Remove and let cool. Remove hazelnut skins by bundling them in a kitchen towel and massing the bundle.

Transfer to a food processor and process to a smooth paste. Add all other ingredients for the chocolate cream and process the mixture until well blended. Transfer to an airtight container or glass jar and store it in the fridge.

Enjoy!

# Section 2: Cake recipes

## 1. Coconut Almond Cake

A creamy cake with almond topping that is ready in 1 hour.

Batter:
1 cup **coconut flour**
1 tsp **cinnamon** (ground)
8 large pastured **eggs**
1 tsp **baking soda**
4 oz. (125 ml) **almond milk yoghurt**
5 tbs **coconut oil** (melted)
½ cup **raw honey**
1 tbs **vanilla extract**
½ tsp **sea salt**

Topping:
1 ½ cups **almonds**
2 tsp **cinnamon**
4 tbs **raw honey**
4 tbs **coconut oil** (cubed)

Makes 6 servings
Calories: 342 per serving

Preheat oven to 325°F (160°F) and place a rack in the middle.
Lightly grease an 8 x 8 inch (20 x 20 cm) baking dish.

Place all batter ingredients into a food processor. Process until
smooth. Transfer to the prepared baking dish. Clean the food
processor and process the topping ingredients until almonds are
coarsely chopped. Spread topping on the batter and bake for 45
minutes, or until golden brown. Remove and let cool.

## 2. Apple Cinnamon Cake

Surprisingly soft and delicious bread, baked using almond flour and arrowroot powder. It is ready in 25 minutes.

2 cups **almond meal**
1 tsp **cinnamon**
½ cup **raw honey**
1 **apple** (peeled, diced)
½ tsp **baking soda**
¼ cup **arrowroot powder**
¼ cup **coconut oil** (melted)
1 pastured **egg**
1 tbs **vanilla extract**
½ tsp **sea salt**

Makes 12 servings
Calories: 215 per serving

Preheat oven to 350°F (180 °C).

In a bowl, combine dry ingredients. Mix well and set aside. In another bowl, mix the wet ingredients until well blended. Gradually pour mixture into the flour mixture, while mixing until a batter is formed.

Transfer the batter into the greased loaf pan and bake for about 30 minutes. Remove and allow to cool on a wire rack.

Enjoy!

# 3. Honey Cake with Raisins

A sweet cake with raisins and honey.

2 ½ cups **almond flour**
½ tsp **Celtic sea salt**
1 tsp **baking soda**
1 tbs **cinnamon**
1½ cup **raw honey**
¼ tsp **cloves**
½ cup organic **vegetable shortening**
4 **pastured eggs**
½ cup **raisins**

Makes 8 servings
Calories: 322 per serving.

Preheat oven to 350 °F (180 °C). Lightly oil and flour-dust an 8-inch (20 cm) cake pan.

In a large bowl, combine almond flour, cinnamon, salt, baking soda, and cloves. Mix well to blend.

In a separate bowl, mix eggs, honey, and shortening until smooth. Add this mixture to the first bowl and mix until batter is formed. Fold in raisins.

Transfer the batter to the cake pan and bake for about 30 minutes, or until toothpick comes out clean when inserted at the center. Remove from the oven and let cool on a wire rack.

# 4. Pumpkin Almond Cake

This luscious pumpkin cake is perfect for Halloween parties or Thanksgiving. It takes about 45 minutes to make.

The Cake:
1 cup **pumpkin puree**
2 large **pastured eggs**
1 cup **almond butter**
¼ cup **raw honey**
1 ½ tsp **baking powder**
1 tsp **vanilla extract**
1 tsp **cinnamon**
½ tsp **baking soda**
¼ tsp **cloves**
1 tsp **ground ginger**
¼ tsp **nutmeg**
½ tsp **lemon zest**

The Frosting:
1/3 cup **coconut butter**
½ cup **coconut oil**
½ tbs **raw honey**
1 tsp **vanilla extract**
10 **Almonds**

Makes 10 servings
Calories: 358 per serving

Preheat oven to 350°F (180°C). Grease an 8 inch (20 cm) baking dish.

In a bowl, combine all of the cake ingredients. Mix to blend. Transfer to the prepared baking dish and bake for about 30 minutes. Remove and let cool on a wire rack.

For the frosting: Place coconut butter and oil in a bowl and heat it over hot water or inside a microwave until softened, but not entirely melted. Add honey, and vanilla extract to the bowl and whisk with a hand mixer until fluffy.

Slice cake into 10 wedges. Spread frosting on top of each wedge and place an almond on it. Loosely cover with plastic wrap and chill.

Enjoy!

# 5. Layered Fruit Cake with Walnut Topping

A fruit cake with walnut and coconut topping. It is ready in 1 hour.

¾ cup + 2 tbs **coconut flour**
¼ cup + ½ cup **coconut butter**
**Coconut oil** (for greasing)
¾ cup **walnuts** (chopped)
¼ cup + 3 tbs **raw honey**
1 tsp **cinnamon**
1 medium **apple** (peeled, thinly sliced)
2 medium **pears** (peeled, thinly sliced)
2 tsp **lemon juice**
5 large **pastured eggs**
1 tsp **vanilla extract**
¼ cup **arrowroot** powder
¾ cup **coconut milk**
¾ tsp **baking** powder
½ tsp **baking** soda
½ tsp **sea salt**

Makes 12 servings
Calories: 292 per serving

Preheat the oven to 350 °F (180 °C). Grease a 9-inch (23 cm) springform pan with coconut oil and line it with foil.

In a bowl, combine cinnamon, walnuts, and honey. Set aside. In another small bowl, mix ¾ cup flour and ¼ cup butter until a crumbly mixture is attained. Fold in the walnut-cinnamon mixture from before and set aside.

In large bowl, combine fruits with the lemon juice. Set aside. In another bowl, combine remaining butter, honey, and eggs. Whisk until blended. Slowly add the remaining flour and the rest of the ingredients. Mixing after each addition until a batter is formed.

Spread half of the batter on the bottom of the pan. Layer the fruit mixture on the top. Spread the remaining batter over the fruit and top with the walnut-cinnamon mixture.

Bake for about 50 minutes, or until toothpick comes out clean if inserted at the center. Remove and let cool on a wire rack. Slice into 12 wedges and serve.

Enjoy!

# 6. Carrot Cake with Raisins

This cake is filled with ingredients that make it soft, healthy and give it a nice odor that fills your home with taste. It is ready in 1 hour and 25 minutes.

1 cup **almond flour**
1/3 cup **coconut flour**
1/3 cup **tapioca powder**
1 tbs **cinnamon** (ground)
½ cup **coconut sugar**
1 tsp **baking powder**
1 tsp **baking soda**
1 tbs **cocoa powder**
½ tsp **salt**
1 ½ tbs **raw honey**
¼ cup **coconut oil** (melted)
4 **pastured eggs** (beaten)
1 **orange** (juiced, zested)
1 ½ tsp **lemon zest** (grated)
¼ cup **pecans** (chopped)
2 cups **carrots** (grated)
5 **figs** (dried, chopped)
½ cup **raisins**
2 tbs **poppy seeds**

Makes 12 servings
Calories: 285 per serving

Preheat oven to 350°F (180°C). Lightly grease a 9 inch (23 cm) Bundt pan.
In a bowl, combine flours, coconut sugar, cinnamon, cocoa, baking powder, baking soda and salt. Mix well.

In another bowl, combine honey with oil, eggs and orange juice. Whip until blended. Add this mixture to first bowl. Mix until a batter is formed. If needed, add water to attain desired consistency. Add the rest of the ingredients and mix until well incorporated. Add more water, if needed.

Bake for about 70 minutes, or until a toothpick comes out clean if inserted at the center. Remove and let cool on wire rack. Slice into 12 wedges and serve.

Enjoy!

# Section 3: Pie recipes

## 1. Lime Pie

A tasty lime pie with an almond-dates crust and tangy coconut milk filling. It is done in about 1 hour.

Crust:
4 pitted **dates**
1 ½ cups whole **almonds**
1 tbs **coconut oil**

Filling:
2 tbs **coconut flour**
1 cup **coconut milk**
½ cup **lime juice**
4 tsp **lime zest**
3 tbs **raw honey**
3 pastured **eggs** (beaten)

Makes 8 servings
Calories: 345 per serving

Preheat oven to 350°F (180°C). Lightly grease a 9 inch (23 cm) pie pan.

In a food processor, combine almonds, dates, and coconut oil. Process until just short of having a nut-butter consistency.

Spread mixture in the bottom and sides of the prepared pie pan. Bake for about 7 minutes or until light brown.

Meanwhile, prepare filling. In a bowl, combine all filling ingredients and mix with a hand mixer, until well blended. Evenly spread into freshly baked pie crust and bake for another 25-30 minutes, or until well set. Remove and let cool on a wire rack.

# 2. Paleo Cheese Sauce Replacement

This is a paleo replacement for cheese sauce, which is needed for recipe 3 and 4 on the next two pages, but can be used for all kinds of recipes.

½ cup **coconut butter** (softened)
3 tbs **coconut milk**
1 ½ tbs **lemon juice**
2 tbs **nutritional yeast**
½ clove **garlic** (crushed)
5 tbs **carrot** (finely grated)
½ cup **coconut oil** (melted)
½ tsp **sea salt**

Makes 1 cup
Calories: 154 per cup

In a heavy duty blender, combine the first 6 ingredients. Blend until smooth.

Gradually add the carrots and coconut oil while blending. Pour the mixture into a shallow container and refrigerate until needed.

Enjoy!

## 3. Chicken Pot Pie

A chicken pot pie made with coconut and tapioca flours, using the paleo cheese from recipe 2a on the previous page. It is ready in 45 minutes.

2 cups **chicken** (cooked)
1 tbs **olive oil**
3 celery **ribs** (diced)
2 **leeks** (chopped)
½ **shallot** (minced)
½ cup **chicken stock**
¼ cup **coconut milk**
1 tbs **tapioca flour**
1/3 cup **tapioca flour**
1/3 cup **coconut flour**
2 tsp **baking soda**
2 **green onions** (chopped)
8 oz. (225 g) dairy-free **cheese** (shredded)
½ cup **water**
**Paleo Cheese Sauce Replacement** (recipe 2)
**Sea salt**

Makes 6 servings
Calories: 210 per serving

Make the paleo cheese sauce replacement from recipe 2, if you have not done so already.

Preheat oven to 350°F (180°C).

In a large saucepan, heat olive oil over medium-high heat. Cook celery, leeks and shallot until tender. Mix in chicken stock, coconut milk, tapioca flour, and chicken. Reduce heat to medium and continue until cooked through. Season with salt to taste.

In a bowl, combine flours, green onions, baking soda, and the paleo cheese sauce replacement. Gradually add tablespoons of water while mixing until crumbly.

Evenly spread vegetable mix into a baking dish. Cover everything with the crumbly mixture and bake for about 30 minutes, or until golden brown.

Enjoy!

# 4. Paleo Quiche

This a paleo version of a traditional French pastry. It is ready in just over 1 hour.

Crust:
1 ½ cups whole **almonds**
1 tbs **coconut oil**

Filling:
1 tsp **olive oil**
1 cup **onion** (thinly sliced)
4 **bacon** slices (browned, crumbled)
¾ cup **Cheese Sauce Replacement** (from recipe 2)
3 large pastured **eggs** (beaten)
3 large pastured **egg** whites (beaten)
1 ½ cups **almond milk**
¼ tsp **ground nutmeg**
½ tsp **salt**
¼ tsp **black pepper** (ground)

Makes 6 servings
Calories: 275 per serving

Make the paleo cheese sauce replacement from recipe 2, if you have not done so already.

Preheat oven to 350°F (180°C).

Make the crust. Process almonds and oil in a food processor until just pureed. Rub a 9 inch (23 cm) pie pan with some coconut oil. Evenly spread and press mixture on the inside of the pan. Bake for about 8 minutes or until just browned.

In a pan, heat oil over medium-high heat. Add onions and sauté for about 8 minutes. Transfer to a bowl and let cool. Evenly distribute onions, bacon, and cheese sauce replacement into the crust. Set aside.

In a bowl, whisk eggs and egg white until smooth. Mix in milk and the remaining ingredients until blended. Pour into the crust, covering the onion mixture.

Bake for about 50 minutes. Loosely cover with tin foil at half time to avoid over browning. Remove and let cool on a wire rack.

Enjoy!

# 5. Apple Pie

This Paleo version of classic apple pie consists of almond crust and apple filling.
It is ready in about 1 hour.

Crust:
2 cups **almond flour**
¼ tbs **sea salt**
2 tbs **coconut oil**
1 **pastured egg**

Filling:
2 ½ lbs. (1.13 kg) **apples** (peeled, cut into slices)
½ cup + 2 tbs **coconut sugar**
3 tbs **almond flour**
1 tbs **vanilla extract**
1 tbs **lemon juice**
1 tsp **cinnamon**
1 large **pastured egg white**
2 tbs **fruit jam** (any)

Makes 6 servings
Calories: 273 per serving

Making the crust: In a food processor, combine almond flour and salt. While mixing, slowly add oil and egg, until a batter is formed. Spread batter on the bottom and sides of a 9 inch (23 cm) pie pan. Chill until firm.

Preheat oven to 375°F (190°C).

In a bowl, combine flour with apple slices, ½ cup coconut sugar, cinnamon, and vanilla extract. Toss to coat.

Place the coated apple slices into the crust in a concentric circle pattern. Brush edges with egg white and sprinkle coconut sugar. Bake for about 45 minutes, or until golden brown. Remove and let cool on a wire rack.

Glaze filling with any fruit jam. Slice and serve.

Enjoy!

# 6. Peach Pie

This peach pie features an almond-coconut crust, yogurt filling, and a peach topping. It is ready in about 3 hours.

Crust:
2 tbs **coconut butter** (melted)
1 ¼ cups **almond meal**
1 large **pastured egg white** (lightly beaten)
1 tbs **olive oil**

Filling:
2 tsp unflavored **gelatin**
1/3 cup **coconut sugar**
1/8 tsp **sea salt**
1 cup **almond milk (**divided)
1 ½ cups **coconut milk yogurt**

Topping:
1 ½ lbs. (680 g) **peaches** (cut into wedges)
2 tbs **water**
2 tsp **lemon juice**
1 tsp **coconut butter** (diced)
2 tbs **coconut sugar**

Makes 12 servings
Calories: 193 per serving

Start with the filling 2 hours before doing the rest.

In a pan, mix gelatin with ½ cup almond milk and let it stand for 3 minutes. Dissolve gelatin over medium heat. Transfer melted gelatin to a bowl and add the rest of the filling ingredients. Mix well to blend. Pour mixture into cooled crust and chill for no less than 2 hours.

Preheat oven to 350°F (180°C).

Make the crust: Process all ingredients in a food processor until well blended. Spread and press mixture into bottom and sides of a 9 inch (23 cm) pie pan and bake for about 30 minutes, or until golden brown.

Increase the oven temperature to 425°F (220°C).

Make the topping: Scatter peaches in a baking dish. Drizzle lemon juice and water, shower with coconut sugar and top with coconut butter. Bake for about 18 minutes. Remove and let it cool completely.

Arrange roasted peaches on top of the chilled pie. Slice and serve.

Enjoy!

# Section 4: Cupcake recipes

## 1. Ginger Cupcakes with Paleo Cream

This is a paleo version of classic ginger cupcakes. They are ready in about 30 minutes.

1 cup + 3 tbs **almond flour**
1/3 cup **coconut flour**
1 tsp **ginger** (ground)
¼ tsp **nutmeg** (freshly grated)
¼ tsp **sea salt**
⅛ tsp **baking powder**
¼ tsp **baking soda**
6 tbs **coconut butter**
½ tsp **vanilla extract**
2/3 cup **raw honey**
4 tsp **lemon zest** (finely grated)
1 **pastured egg**
1-inch (2.5 cm) **ginger** (finely grated)
½ cup **paleo cream** (see below)
¼ cup **ginger** (finely chopped)

Paleo Cream:
1 cup **coconut milk** (chilled)
2 tbs **lemon juice** or **apple cider vinegar**
⅛ tsp **sea salt**

Makes 36 mini cupcakes
Calories: 47 per cupcake

Make the paleo cream: Combine cream, lemon juice and salt. Whisk to blend. Adjust to desired taste.

Preheat oven to 350°F (180°C). Line three 12 cup muffin pans with paper liners.

In a bowl, combine flours with nutmeg, ginger, salt, baking soda, and baking powder. Mix well and set aside.

In a bowl, beat butter using a hand mixer until smooth. Add 3 tbs raw honey, vanilla extract, lemon zest and ginger. Beat for about 1 minute. Gradually add more honey and beat after each addition. Add the egg and beat for 1 more minute until very smooth.

Slowly add the flour mixture, paleo cream, and ginger. Mix until well blended.

Transfer mixture to prepared muffin pans until they are ¾ full. Bake for about 18 minutes, or until light brown and fluffy. Remove from the oven and let cool on a wire rack. Remove cupcakes and let cool off completely.

Enjoy!

## 2. Jelly Donut Cupcakes

These cupcakes make use of fruit jam, which means their flavor is easy to vary. They are ready in about 40 minutes.

½ cup **coconut** oil (melted)
½ cup **applesauce**
3 tbs **raw honey**
1 tbs **vanilla extract**
3 **pastured eggs**
½ cup **coconut flour**
1 tbs **almond milk**
¼ tsp **baking soda**
½ cup **fruit jam** (any)
½ tsp **sea salt**

Makes 12 cupcakes
Calories: 178 per cup cake

Preheat oven to 350°F (180°C). Prepare parchment paper-lined 12 muffin cups.

In a food processor, combine coconut oil, applesauce, eggs, vanilla extract and raw honey. Process until well blended. Transfer to a bowl, gradually add flour, baking soda and salt. Mix until a batter is formed. If needed, add more almond milk to attain desired consistency.

Spoon batter into muffin cups until they are ¾ full. Add spoonful portions of any fruit jam (apricot, raspberry etc.) to each cup and swirl to mix slightly. Bake for about 25 minutes, or until toothpick comes out clean if inserted at the center.

# 3. Vanilla Cupcakes

These vanilla cupcakes are ready in 45 minutes.

1 ¼ cups **almond flour**
½ cup **coconut flour**
1 ½ tsp **baking powder**
½ tsp **sea salt**
3 tbs **coconut butter** (softened)
1 cup **raw honey**
3 tbs **coconut oil**
4 **pastured eggs**
½ cup **applesauce**
½ cup **almond milk**
½ tsp **vanilla extract**

Makes 12 cupcakes
Calories: 76 per serving

Preheat oven to 350°F (180°C). Prepare 12 cup muffin pans lined with paper liners.

In a bowl, mix flours, baking powder, and salt. Set aside.

Using a hand mixer, beat butter in a bowl for about 3 minutes until smooth. Slowly add ½ of the honey and beat for about 2 minutes. Add oil and remaining honey, beat for another 2 minutes or until light and smooth. One by one, add eggs and beat after each addition. Add applesauce and beat until well blended.

Add the flour mixture, almond milk, and vanilla extract, then beat until fully incorporated.

Fill cups with the batter and bake for about 23 minutes, or until a toothpick comes out clean if inserted at the center of a cupcake. Remove from the oven and let cool completely.

# 4. Almond-Banana Cupcakes

These cupcakes are colored with natural beet juice and frosted with dairy-free yogurt. They are ready in 35 minutes.

Cupcakes:
1 cup **almond flour**
¼ cup **coconut flour**
¾ cup **coconut sugar**
1/3 cup **cocoa powder**
1 tsp **baking soda**
2 **pastured eggs** (beaten)
1 tbs **vanilla** extract
½ tsp **beet juice**
1/3 cup **banana** (mashed)
1 cup **almond milk**
1 tsp **apple cider vinegar**
½ tsp **sea salt**

Frosting:
1 cup **almond milk yogurt**
3 tbs **raw honey**
½ tsp **vanilla extract**

Makes 12 cupcakes
Calories: 67 per serving

Preheat oven to 350°F (180°C). Prepare 12 cup muffin pan lined with paper liners.

In a large bowl, combine flours along with all other dry cupcake ingredients. Set aside.

In another bowl, beat the eggs. Add the remaining ingredients. Mix well to blend, then transfer to the flour mixture. Mix until well incorporated and a batter is formed.

Fill muffin cups with the batter and bake for 20-25 minutes, or until a toothpick comes out clean when inserted at the center of a cupcake. Remove and let cool on a wire rack.

In a bowl, whisk all frosting ingredients together until smooth. Spread on top of each cupcake.

Enjoy!

# 5. Paleo Chocolate Cupcakes

This is a chocolate dessert made with coconut flour, coconut oil and pastured eggs. It uses a glazing made in recipe 5 of section 1.

½ cup **coconut flour**
¼ cup **cocoa powder**
¼ tsp **sea salt**
½ tsp **baking soda**
3 large **pastured eggs**
4 tbs **coconut oil**
½ cup **honey**
**Hot chocolate** (recipe 5, section 1, optional)

Makes 10 servings
Calories: 69 per serving

If you wish to use the hot chocolate glazing, prepare it according to recipe 5 of section 1.

Preheat oven to 350°F (180°C). Prepare a 12 cup muffin pan lined with paper liners.

In a bowl, combine all dry ingredients and mix well. In separate bowl, whisk eggs, oil, and honey until smooth.

Slowly add the dry mixture while mixing, until a batter is formed. Fill muffin cups with batter and bake for about 20 minutes. Remove from the oven and let cool on a wire rack.

Optionally, top cupcakes with the hot chocolate.

Enjoy!

# Section 5: Cookie recipes

## 1. Fruity Almond Cookies

These are very light cookies with applesauce, cranberries and pecans. They are ready in 25 minutes.

3 cups **almond flour**
1 tbs **coconut oil**
2 cups **applesauce**
1 ½ tsp **baking soda**
½ cup **coconut sugar**
½ cup **pecans** (chopped)
½ cup **cranberries** (dried)
2 **pastured eggs** (beaten)
¼ cup **coconut flour**
2 tsp **cinnamon** (ground)

Makes 24 cookies
Calories: 113 per serving

Preheat oven to 400°F (200°C). Prepare 2 baking sheets lined with paper liners and lightly brushed with coconut oil.

In a bowl, dissolve baking soda in applesauce. Gradually add the rest of the ingredients. Mix after adding each ingredient and continue until a smooth batter is formed.

Drop spoonful portions on the prepared baking sheet, lightly press each cookie and bake for about 15 minutes. Remove and let cool on a wire rack.

Enjoy!

## 2. Pumpkin Cookies

These pumpkin cookies are perfect for Halloween and
Thanksgiving. They are prepared and baked in about 40 minutes.

2 cups **almond meal**
½ tsp **baking soda**
½ cup **coconut oil** (melted)
½ cup **pumpkin puree**
1 tbs **pumpkin pie spice**
½ tsp **sea salt**
¼ cup unsweetened **coconut** (shredded)
1 tbs pure **vanilla extract**
½ cup **raw honey**

Makes 15 servings
Calories: 85 per serving

Preheat oven to 350°F (180°C). Line a baking sheet with
parchment paper.

In a bowl, combine all ingredients and blend using a hand mixer
until a batter has formed. Drop 1-tbs-portions of batter onto
prepared baking sheet and bake for about 30 minutes. Remove
and let cool on a wire rack.

Enjoy!

# 3. Macadamia Chocolate Cookies

In this recipe, macadamia is turned into nut butter and baked with coconut flour and chocolate chips. These cookies take about 40 minutes to make.

2 tbs **coconut flour**
1 cup **macadamia nut butter**
¼ cup **coconut oil**
1 tsp **vanilla extract**
¼ cup **raw honey**
1 **pastured egg**
½ cup **dark chocolate chips**
1 pinch of **sea salt**

Macadamia nut butter
6 tbs **coconut oil**
1 lb. **macadamia nuts**
1 pinch **sea salt**
5 tbs raw **honey** (optional)

Makes 8 servings
Calories: 97 per serving

Preheat oven to 350°F (180°C). Line 2 baking sheets with parchment paper.

In a food processor, combine all ingredients for the macadamia nut butter and process to desired consistency.

In a bowl, combine nut butter with coconut oil, honey, vanilla and egg. Blend with a hand mixer until a smooth batter has formed. Fold in chocolate chips. Chill for about 15 minutes.

Drop 2-tbs-portions of batter on prepared baking sheets and bake for 15 minutes. Remove and let cool on a wire rack. Serve warm.

# 4. Honey Coconut Macaroons

This recipe contains only 4 ingredients, but represents a great treat for coconut lovers. It is ready in about 40 minutes.

2 large **egg whites**
¼ cup **raw honey**
¼ tsp **sea salt**
2 ½ cups **coconut flakes**

Makes 8 servings
Calories: 86 per serving

Preheat oven to 350°F (180°C). Line a baking sheet with parchment paper.

In a bowl, whisk egg whites with honey and salt until smooth. Add coconut flakes, mix until incorporated. Refrigerate for about 30 minutes.

Drop 2-tbs-portions of batter onto prepared baking sheet and bake for about 10 minutes, or until golden brown. Remove and let cool on a wire rack.

Enjoy!

# 5. Chocolate Carrot Cookies

These cookies can be prepared and baked in 40 minutes.

1 cup **coconut flour**
½ cup **tapioca flour**
2 large **carrots** (shredded)
1 cup **coconut sugar**
1 cup **coconut oil** (melted)
2 **pastured eggs** (beaten)
1 tsp **vanilla**
½ tsp **pumpkin pie spice**
**Sea salt** (to taste)
½ cup **chocolate chips**
    or self-made **paleo chocolate**

Makes 12 servings
Calories: 186 per serving

Preheat oven to 350°F (180°C). Line a cookie sheet with parchment paper.

Whisk eggs in a bowl, then add oil, coconut sugar and vanilla extract. Mix to blend.
Add carrots, flours and spices. Mix well. Fold in chocolate chips or the self-made paleo chocolate from recipe 1, section 1.

Spoon batter onto prepared baking sheet, press to flatten and bake for about 30 minutes. Remove and let cool on a wire rack.

Enjoy!

# Section 6: Frozen Desserts

## 1. Banana Pecan Ice Cream

This quick treat is ready in just 5 minutes.

2 **bananas** (chopped, frozen)
1 tbs **raw honey**
1 tsp **vanilla extract**
1 pinch **sea salt**
½ cup **pecans**

Makes 2 servings
Calories: 142 per serving

Partially thaw bananas. Transfer to a food processor along with honey, vanilla and salt. Process to puree. Add pecans and pulse to desired nut sizes. Serve immediately.

Enjoy!

## 2. Paleo Banana-Chocolate Ice Cream

This ice cream recipe is a real treat and uses the paleo mousse chocolate of recipe 6 in section 1.

2 ripe **bananas** (chopped, frozen)
1/3 cup **paleo mousse chocolate**
**Cocoa nibs** (for garnish)

Makes 2 servings
Calories: 143 per serving

Make the paleo mousse chocolate as described in recipe 6 of section 1. The mousse needs to be cool, so it should be refrigerated before you go on.

Slightly thaw frozen bananas. Transfer to a food processor along with the mousse chocolate. Process until desired ice cream consistency is attained.

Garnish with cocoa nibs and serve immediately.

Enjoy!

# 3. Strawberry Sorbet

A quick and easy sorbet that is ready in 25 minutes. It can be varied by using other types of berries.

2 cups **strawberries** (cut tops)
¼ cup **almond milk**
**Mint**

Makes 4 servings
Calories: 72 per serving

Puree strawberries in a food processor. Add almond milk and some mint, then process until the mixture is well blended.

Transfer to the freezer and wait for about 20 minutes, or until desired thickness is attained. Serve and enjoy!

Enjoy!

# 4. Creamy Berry Smoothie

This smoothie is perfect on hot days. It is made with almond milk yogurt and takes 2 minutes to be ready.

2 cups **orange juice**
1 cup **almond milk yogurt**
2 small **ripe bananas**
¼ tsp **vanilla**
1 cup **any berries** (fresh or frozen)

Makes 4 servings
Calories: 91 per serving

Simply blend all ingredients in a food processor until smooth.

Enjoy!

## 5. Pumpkin Ice Cream

A pumpkin ice cream with creamy coconut milk. Like all pumpkin recipes, this is perfect for Halloween or Thanksgiving.

1 cup **coconut milk**
¼ cup **raw honey**
½ tbs **pumpkin pie spice**
½ cup **pumpkin (pureed)**
1 tsp **vanilla extract**
½ cup **pecans**
**Cinnamon** (ground)

Makes 4 servings
Calories: 172 per serving

Combine all ingredients in a food processor and process until desired chunkiness of pecans is reached.

Transfer the mixture to an ice cream machine and use it according to its instructions.

Sprinkle with cinnamon.

Enjoy!

# Section 7: Muffin and Waffle Recipes

## 1. Pumpkin Muffins

Delicious pumpkin muffins that are ready in 35 minutes.

1 ½ cups **almond flour**
1 tsp **baking powder**
1 tsp **baking soda**
½ tsp **cinnamon** (ground)
1 ½ tsp **pumpkin pie spice**
1/8 tsp **sea salt**
¾ cup **canned pumpkin**
3 large **eggs**
¼ cup **raw honey**
2 tsp **almond butter**
2 tbs **almonds** (slivered)

Makes 6 servings
Calories: 97 per serving

Preheat oven to 350°F (180°C). Lightly grease muffin cups.

In a bowl, combine flour with the next 6 ingredients.

In a separate bowl, beat eggs, honey and almond butter until smooth. Transfer to the flour mixture. Mix until batter is formed.

Bake for about 25 minutes on the middle rack, or until golden brown. Remove from the oven and sprinkle almonds on top. Let muffins cool before serving.

## 2. Paleo Spinach Muffins

These egg muffins are made with almond milk and dairy-free cheese. They are ready in 35 minutes.

8 large **eggs**
½ cup **almond milk**
1 cup **dairy-free cheese** (shredded)
1 cup **spinach** (shredded)
**Sea salt** and ground **black pepper**
1 tbs **coconut butter**
**Fresh basil** (minced)

Makes 4 servings
Calories: 214 per serving

Preheat oven to 350°F (180°C). Lightly grease a 12-cup muffin pan.

In a bowl, beat eggs and milk. Add the rest of the ingredients and season with salt and pepper. Mix until a batter has formed.

Fill muffin cups with batter and bake for about 30 minutes, or until golden brown. Remove and let cool on a wire rack.

Enjoy!

# 3. Coconut-Banana-Strawberry Waffles

These coconut-banana-strawberry waffles are perfect on a cold winter evening.

½ cup **coconut flour**
¼ tsp **baking soda**
¼ cup **coconut milk**
8 **pastured eggs**
½ cup **coconut butter**
¼ tsp **sea salt**

Topping
2 sliced **strawberries**
1 tbs **almond butter**
½ **small banana**
2 tsp **raw honey**

Makes 4 servings
Calories: 102 per serving

Preheat a waffle maker.

In a food processor, combine all ingredients. Process until a batter has formed. Transfer batter to the waffle maker and use it according to the instruction manual.

Serve topped with almond butter, mashed strawberries and banana slices. Drizzle raw honey on top.

Enjoy!

## 4. Omelet Bacon Waffles

This recipe sandwiches omelet and bacon in between waffles, which is perfect for breakfast. It is done in 12 minutes.

Waffle:
1 cup **almond flour**
½ cup **tapioca flour**
2 tbs **coconut flour**
1 tsp **baking soda**
½ tsp **sea salt**
4 **pastured eggs**
1/3 cup **coconut milk**
2 tbs **coconut oil**
2 tsp **vanilla extract**

Topping
2 slices **bacon**
2 tsp **olive oil** (divided)
2 **pastured eggs**
2 tbs **chives** (chopped)
¼ tsp **pepper**
¼ cup **raw honey**

Makes 4 servings
Calories: 174 per serving

In a large bowl, combine all dry waffle ingredients. Mix well and set aside.

In another bowl, beat eggs, then add the rest of the wet waffle ingredients and mix until well blended. Slowly pour flour mixture into the wet mixture, Mix until a batter has formed. Let it stand for about 5 minutes.

Transfer batter to the waffle maker and use it according to the instruction manual.

Preheat oven to 400°F (200°C).

In a saucepan, heat oil over medium-high heat. Add bacon and brown for about 3 minutes. Drain on paper towel-lined plate.

For the topping: In a bowl, beat eggs, then add chives and pepper. Mix to blend. Add more oil to the saucepan and stir-fry egg mixture over medium-low flame for about 5 minutes, or until well cooked.

Place 4 waffles on a baking sheet. Layer ¼ of the scrambled eggs, bacon, and dairy-free cheese on each of the waffles. Top each waffle with the remaining 4 waffles.

Transfer to the oven and bake for about 4 minutes, or until crisp.

Drizzle honey and serve immediately.

Enjoy!

# 5. Banana-Cinnamon Waffles

Another waffle recipe that is perfect for cold winter evenings.

2 tsp **cinnamon** (ground)
1 tsp **sea salt**
4 **pastured eggs**
¼ cup **almond flour**
½ cup **coconut flour**
½ cup **tapioca flour**
1 large **banana**
1 cup **coconut milk**
1/3 cup **coconut oil** (melted)
2 tsp. **vanilla extract**
2 tbs **raw honey**

Makes 4 servings
Calories: 125 per serving

Preheat a waffle maker.

In a food processor, combine all ingredients. Process until a batter has formed.

Transfer batter to the waffle maker and use it according to the instruction manual.

Enjoy!

# Section 8: Bread and Buns

## 1. Flaxseed Bread

This delicious bread is made with a combination of coconut and almond flours. It goes very well with homemade fruit jam.

2 tbs **coconut flour**
1 ½ cups **almond flour**
¼ cup **golden flaxseed**
1 ½ tsp **baking soda**
¼ cup **coconut oil**
1 tbs **raw honey**
5 **pastured eggs**
1 tbs **apple cider vinegar**
¼ tsp **sea salt**

Makes 8 servings
Calories: 243 per serving

Preheat the oven to 350°F (180°C). Lightly grease a loaf pan with coconut oil.

In a food processor, combine all dry ingredients. Pulse to blend. Gradually add in wet ingredients while pulsing until a batter is formed.

Evenly spread batter into the prepared loaf pan and bake for about 30 minutes. Remove and let cool on a wire rack.

Enjoy!

## 2. Pumpkin-Blueberry Bread

A pumpkin bread that is perfect for Halloween and Thanksgiving.
It is ready in about 1 hour.

½ cup **macadamia nuts**
1 cup **cashew nuts**
**Macadamia nut oil**
1 cup **pumpkin puree**
1 cup **almond meal**
1 ripe **banana** (chopped)
1 tsp **baking powder**
2 **pastured eggs**
1 tsp **baking soda**
2 tsp **cinnamon**
½ tsp **pumpkin pie spice**
**Coconut oil** (for greasing)
1 cup **blueberries**
1 pinch **sea salt**

Makes 12 slices
Calories: 92 per slice

Preheat oven to 375°F (190 °C).

In a food processor, combine cashews and macadamia nuts.
Process into a fine
nut meal. Add macadamia nut oil while processing until a smooth
butter is attained. Add in bananas and pumpkin puree and mix
until a thick batter is formed.

In a large bowl, beat eggs. Add banana-nut mixture and the rest of
the ingredients except for the berries. Mix well until fully
incorporated. Fold in the berries.

Lightly oil a bread pan and evenly spread batter into it. Transfer to the oven and bake for about 50 minutes, or until toothpick comes out clean when inserted at the center. Remove and let cool for 10 minutes before serving.

Enjoy!

## 3. Banana Bread

A delicious banana bread with chocolate and cinnamon. It is ready in about 1 hour.

Chocolate swirl:
1 cup **dark chocolate** (cut into chunks)
1 tsp **coconut oil**
1 tbs **coconut butter**
2 tbs **cinnamon**

Banana bread:
4 ripe medium **bananas**
½ cup **coconut flour**
1 tsp **baking soda**
½ cup **almond butter**
4 large **pastured eggs**
**Coconut oil** (for greasing)
1/8 tsp **sea salt**

Makes 6 servings
Calories: 295 per serving

For the chocolate swirl: Place chocolate chunks, butter and coconut oil in a bowl. Place the bowl over a pot with simmering water to melt the ingredients. Mix to blend. Add cinnamon and mix again. Set aside.

For the banana bread: Preheat the oven to 350°F (180°C). Lightly grease a loaf pan with coconut oil.

In a large bowl, mash bananas, then add flour, baking powder and salt. Mix to blend.

In a separate bowl, beat eggs with almond butter until creamy. Pour into the banana mixture and mix well.

Transfer ½ of this mixture to the prepared pan, add 2 tbs of melted chocolate mixture and swirl with a fork. Pour the remaining banana mixture and add another chocolate mix. Swirl to form patterns.

Bake for about 50 minutes, or until knife comes out clear when inserted at the center. Remove and let cool before serving.

Enjoy!

## 4. Fluffy White Bread

This white bread is ready in just over 2 hours.

¼ cup **coconut flour**
½ cup **tapioca flour**
1 cup **arrowroot powder**
2 tbs **coconut sugar**
1 ¾ cup **almond flour**
2 ½ tsp **dry yeast**
1 tbs **flaxseeds** (ground)
3 **pastured eggs**
¼ cup + 1 ½ tsp **olive oil**
1 ½ cups **water** (warm)
1 ½ tsp **sea salt**

Makes 8 servings
Calories: 241 per serving

In a bowl, combine all dry ingredients. Mix well and set aside.

In another bowl, whisk eggs with ¼ cup of the oil and water. Pour into the previous bowl and mix until a soft batter is formed. Add more water if needed to attain desired consistency. Set aside for 1 hour.

Preheat the oven to 350°F (180°C). Lightly grease a loaf pan with oil.

Evenly spread batter into the prepared pan and bake for about 55 minutes. Loosely cover with tin foil after 10 minutes to avoid excessive browning. Remove and let cool on wire rack.

Enjoy!

# 5. Fruity Muesli Bread

This fruity and nutty bread is ready in just over 1 hour.

4 **pastured eggs**
¾ cup **almond butter**
1 tbs **raw honey**
1 tsp **ground flax meal**
¼ cup **arrowroot flour**
¼ cup **almond flour**
¼ cup **apricots** (dried, chopped)
½ cup **pistachios** (chopped)
¼ cup **hazelnuts** (chopped)
½ tsp **baking soda**
1½ cup **cranberries** (dried)
¼ cup **sesame seeds**
¼ cup **sunflower seeds**
1 tsp **sea salt**

Makes 6 servings (about 12 slices)
Calories: 152 per serving

Preheat the oven to 350°F (180°C). Grease a loaf pan and lightly coat with almond flour.

In a bowl, combine almond butter, honey, and eggs. Whisk until smooth. Set aside.

In another bowl, combine flours, meals, baking soda and salt. Mix well. Gradually pour into the wet mixture and mix until fully incorporated. Fold in nuts, seeds and fruits.

Evenly spread batter into the prepared pan and bake for about 1 hour, or until toothpick comes out clean when inserted at the center. Remove and let cool on a wire rack.

# Section 9: Bagels, Pretzels, Tortillas

## 1. Coconut Bagels with Seeds

These delicious seed bagels take about 25 minutes to make.

¼ cup **sunflower seeds**
¼ cup **pumpkin seeds**
1 tbs **arrowroot powder**
½ tsp **unrefined sea salt**
2 tbs **coconut flour**
1 tbs **hemp seeds**
2 tsp **poppy seeds**
½ tsp **cream of tartar**
¼ tsp **baking soda**
4 **pastured eggs**
3 tbs **coconut oil**

Makes 6 bagels
Calories: 98 per bagel

Preheat the oven to 350°F (180°C). Grease a donut pan with coconut oil.

In a food processor, combine sunflower and pumpkin seeds and process to coarse bits. Add the rest of the dry ingredients and pulse several times to combine.

In a large bowl, whisk eggs with coconut oil. Add the contents of the food processor and mix until a batter has formed. Set aside for a couple of minutes. Add more water if needed to attain desired consistency.

Fill donut cups with batter and bake for about 15 minutes, or until edges start to brown. Remove and let cool on a wire rack.

## 2. Pumpkin Bagels

These pumpkin bagels take about 35 minutes to make.

1/3 cup **coconut flour**
3 tbs **golden flax meal**
½ tsp **cinnamon**
1 ¼ tsp **pumpkin pie spice**
3 **pastured eggs** (beaten)
2 tbs **coconut oil** (melted)
¼ cup **almond milk**
½ cup **pumpkin puree**
1 tsp **vanilla extract**
1½ tbs **raw honey**
½ tsp **baking soda**
1 tsp **apple cider vinegar**
⅛ tsp **sea salt**

Makes 8 bagels
Calories: 92 per bagel

Preheat the oven to 350°F (180°C). Grease a donut pan with coconut oil.

In a bowl, combine all of the dry ingredients, except the baking soda. Mix well and set aside.

In a separate bowl, whisk eggs. Add the rest of the wet ingredients and baking soda. Mix to blend. Pour the wet mixture into the flour mixture and stir until a batter has formed.

Scoop batter into the prepared donut pan. Bake for about 25 minutes or until browned. Remove and let cool on a wire rack.

Enjoy!

## 3. Soft Pretzels

These pretzels are both delicious and crunchy. They are ready in 30 minutes.

3 cups **tapioca starch**
2 cups **coconut flour**
1 tbs active **dry yeast**
1 ½ cup **warm water**
1/3 cup **coconut sugar**
4 tbs **baking soda**
**Sea salt** (to taste)

Makes 6 servings
Calories: 45 per serving

Preheat oven to 475°F (250 °C).

In a bowl, dissolve yeast in warm water. Add flour and coconut sugar, then mix until a batter has formed. Roll batter to form elongated thin rolls and form the traditional pretzel forms.

Fill a saucepan with 2 cups of water. Dissolve baking soda and bring to a boil over medium-high heat.

Dip pretzels into boiling water for about 15 seconds, or until golden. Place pretzels on a salted baking sheet, sprinkle salt and bake for about 10 minutes, or until golden brown.

Enjoy!

# 4. Paleo Tortillas

These paleo tortillas are ready in 30 minutes.

¼ cup **coconut flour**
¾ cup **almond flour**
½ cup **tapioca flour**
½ cup **tapioca starch**
1 tsp **baking powder**
¼ cup **coconut butter**
1 cup **warm water**
1 tsp **sea salt**

Makes 10 servings
Calories: 89 per serving

In a bowl, combine all dry ingredients. Add coconut butter and mix until crumbly. Add ½ cup of warm water and mix. Gradually add more water while mixing until a smooth batter is formed.

Form 8 dough balls, cover with a moist towel and work on them one ball at a time. Roll each into a circular disc, 6 inch (15 cm) in diameter. Cook in a hot skillet for several seconds until bubbly. Flip and cook the other side.

Enjoy!

# 5. Spiced Paleo Tortillas

These chili tortillas take 20 minutes to make.

6 **egg whites**
4 tbs **coconut flour**
4 tbs **almond milk**
½ tsp **cumin** (ground)
½ tsp **chili powder**
¼ tsp **garlic salt**
½ tsp **sea salt**

Makes 8 servings
Calories: 35 per serving

In a bowl, combine all ingredients. Mix well and set aside for a few minutes. Add more liquid if needed to attain desired soft consistency.

Grease a non-stick skillet with coconut oil and pour batter at the center. Spread batter and make it as thin as possible by tilting the pan until having a diameter of 6 inches (15 cm).

Heat for about 1 minute, or until batter is firm. Flip and cook for about 30 seconds on the other side. Work in batches.

Enjoy!

# Section 10: Pancakes and Brownies

## 1. Paleo Pumpkin Pancakes

Like all pumpkin recipes, these pancakes are perfect for Halloween and Thanksgiving. They are ready in 20 minutes.

½ cup **pumpkin puree**
4 **pastured eggs** (beaten)
1 tsp **vanilla extract**
2 tbs **raw honey**
1 tsp **pumpkin pie spice**
¼ tsp **baking soda**
1 tsp **cinnamon**
2 tbs **coconut oil**

Makes 2 servings
Calories: 110 per serving

In a bowl, whisk the eggs. Add vanilla, honey and pumpkin puree. Mix until smooth. Add baking soda and spices. Mix until well blended.

Grease a non-stick skillet with coconut oil and pour batter at the center. Spread batter and make it as thin as possible by tilting the pan until having a diameter of 6 inches (15 cm).

Heat for about 1 minute, or until batter is firm. Flip and cook for about 30 seconds on the other side. Work in batches.

Serve with honey and coconut oil on top.

Enjoy!

## 2. Almond Blueberry Pancakes

These almond flour pancakes are ready in 20 minutes.

3 large **pastured eggs**
1 tbs **vanilla extract**
2 tbs **raw honey**
1 tbs **water**
1 ½ cups **almond flour**
¼ tsp **baking soda**
1 tbs **olive oil** (plus more as needed)
¼ tsp **sea salt**
**Blueberries, honey, almonds** (for serving)

Makes 2 servings
Calories: 120 per serving

In a bowl, whisk egg until smooth. Add vanilla, honey and water. Mix until blended. Gradually add almond flour, baking soda, and salt. Mix to combine.

Grease a non-stick skillet with oil and pour batter at the center. Spread batter and make it as thin as possible by tilting the pan until having a diameter of 6 inches (15 cm).

Heat for about 1 minute, or until batter is firm. Flip and cook for about 30 seconds on the other side. Work in batches.

Serve with chopped almonds, blueberries, and honey.

Enjoy!

# 3. Carrot Scallion Pancakes

These pancakes are ready in 20 minutes.

3 **scallions** (finely chopped)
½ tsp **coconut flour**
3 cups **carrots** (shredded)
3 **pastured eggs** (whipped)
**Olive oil** (for frying)
½ tsp **sea salt**
**Applesauce** (for serving)

Makes 6 servings
Calories: 96 per serving

In a bowl, mix eggs with carrots, and scallions until well blended. Add salt and flour. Mix until a batter is formed.

Heat oil in a skillet over medium heat. Scoop a tbs-portion of batter into the skillet, spread and cook for about 1 minute per side, or until browned and crisp. Work in batches.

Serve with applesauce and enjoy!

## 4. Choco-Banana Brownie

A Paleo dieter can even enjoy brownies, if the right ingredients are used. These chocolate goodies are ready in 35 minutes.

2 tsp **cocoa powder**
3 tbs **almond flour**
1 tsp **coconut flour**
1 tbs **mashed banana** (mashed)
1 **egg white**
1 tbs **almond milk**
1 tsp **coconut oil** (softened)
1 tsp **dark chocolate chips**

Makes 2 servings
Calories: 142 per serving

Preheat oven to 350°F (180°C). Lightly grease a small baking dish.

In a bowl, combine mashed bananas with egg white, oil and almond milk. Mix until well blended. Add the rest of the ingredients and mix until a batter is formed.

Evenly spread batter into the prepared baking dish and bake for about 25 minutes, or until toothpick comes out clean when inserted at the center.

Enjoy!

# 5. Zucchini Brownies

These flourless brownies combine the taste of zucchini, almond and vanilla. They are ready in 35 minutes.

2 cups **zucchini** (shredded)
1 cup **almond butter**
1 **pastured egg**
1 tsp **vanilla extract**
1 tsp **cinnamon**
½ tsp **nutmeg**
1/3 cup **raw honey**
½ tsp **allspice**
1 tsp **baking soda**

Makes 12 servings
Calories: 121 per serving

Preheat oven to 350°F (180°C). Lightly grease a square baking dish.

In a bowl, combine zucchini with the rest of the ingredients. Mix until well blended.

Spread in the prepared dish and bake for about 25 minutes, or until toothpick comes out clean when inserted at the center.

Enjoy!

Printed in Poland
by Amazon Fulfillment
Poland Sp. z o.o., Wrocław